U.S. Military Forces

U.S. NAVY

LUKE COLINS

BLACK RABBIT BOOKS

Bolt is published by Black Rabbit Books
P.O. Box 3263, Mankato, Minnesota, 56002.
www.blackrabbitbooks.com

Jennifer Besel, editor; Michael Sellner, interior designer;
Catherine Cates, cover designer; Omay Ayres, photo researcher

Library of Congress Cataloging-in-Publication Data
Names: Colins, Luke, author.
Title: U.S. Navy / by Luke Colins.
Other titles: United States Navy
Description: Mankato, Minnesota : Black Rabbit Books, [2021]
Series: Bolt. U.S. Military Forces | Includes bibliographical references and index.
Audience: Ages 8-12 | Audience: Grades 4-6
Summary: "Learn about the powerful sailors who make up the U.S. Navy, including what they do and the training it takes to become one."— Provided by publisher.
Identifiers: LCCN 2019040134 (print) | LCCN 2019040135 (ebook)
ISBN 9781623103002 (hardcover) | ISBN 9781644663967 (paperback)
ISBN 9781623103941 (ebook)
Subjects: LCSH: United States. Navy—Juvenile literature.
Classification: LCC VA58.4 .C65 2021 (print) | LCC VA58.4 (ebook)
DDC 359.00973—dc23
LC record available at https://lccn.loc.gov/2019040134
LC ebook record available at https://lccn.loc.gov/2019040135

Image Credits

commons.m.wikimedia.org: Petty Officer 3rd Class Walter M. Wayman/U.S. Navy, 6–7; commons.wikimedia.org: Mass Communication Specialist 2nd Class Eddie Harrison/U.S. Navy, 8 (weapons); Mass Communication Specialist 2nd Class Eva-Marie Ramsaran/U.S. Navy, 18 (b); Mass Communication Specialist Seaman Cory Rose/ U.S. Navy, 18 (t); Photographer's Mate 3rd Class Lindsay Switzer/U.S. Navy, 10, 11 (t); Photographer's Mate Airman Lamel J. Hinton/U.S. Navy, 11 (b; defense.gov: Navy Petty Officer 2nd Class Scott Swofford/U.S. Navy, 32; dvidshub.net: Aviation Ordnanceman Airman Shawn Murphy, 21 (t); Petty Officer 2nd Class Cameron Stoner/U.S. Navy, 20 (t); navsea.navy.mil: U.S. Navy, 26; navy.mil: Petty Officer 2nd Class Greg Johnson/U.S. Navy, 16 (inset); U.S. Navy, 8 (water), 12 (main), 23 (t); navy.mil/flicker.com: Mass Communication Specialist 2nd Class Kelsey L. Adams/U.S. Navy, Cover (main); navylive.dodlive.mi: Mass Communication Specialist 1st Class James Kimber/U.S. Navy, 23 (b); U.S. Navy, 8 (firefighting); northropgrumman.com: Northrop Grumman, 16–17; photos.usni.org: U.S. Naval Institute, 24–25; Shutterstock: 19srb81, 8 (bkgd); Beautiful landscape, 12–13 (ship); FOTOGRIN, 1, 31; Jason and Bonnie Grower, 3; Neuevector, Cover (wings); Ramunas Bruzas, 14–15 (bkgd); usnhistory.navylive.dodlive.mil: Mass Communication Specialist 3rd Class Spencer Roberts/U.S. Navy, 28–29; usni.org: USNI News, 4–5, 8 (port), 20–21 (main); Every effort has been made to contact copyright holders for material reproduced in this book. Any omissions will be rectified in subsequent printings if notice is given to the publisher.

Contents

123
78

CHAPTER 1

To Protect and Serve

The USS *Theodore Roosevelt* breaks through the ocean waves. It's traveling about 30 miles (48 kilometers) per hour. Sailors onboard get ready. A fighter jet soars toward the aircraft carrier. Controllers on the flight deck make sure the path is clear. Soon the jet roars onto the carrier and makes a safe landing.

Important Roles

The U.S. Navy runs aircraft carriers. It stations these huge ships near areas of **conflict**. Aircraft take off from and land on them.

Running aircraft carriers is just one of the U.S. Navy's jobs. The Navy works from the sea and air to protect the United States. Pilots shoot down enemies. Sailors float submarines into enemy **territory**.

HEAD
102
FLY
ONE

firefighting

water survival

weapons training

getting a ship into and out of port

CHAPTER 2

Training

Sailors don't just jump into work. They have to go through training first. All **recruits** start with boot camp. Recruits must pass this eight-week training to join the Navy. If they can't pass, they are sent home.

What Recruits Learn at Boot Camp

Still Learning

The training doesn't end after boot camp. Immediately after camp, sailors go to A School. At this training, they learn to do specific jobs.

The Navy needs people trained for all kinds of missions. Some sailors learn to be **engineers**. Some study aircraft electronics. Others even train to run **nuclear reactors**.

Many Jobs

installing equipment

fixing electronics

testing water

CHAPTER 3

Jobs and Missions

Sailors spend months at a time at sea. They do jobs all around the world. One of the Navy's biggest jobs is sea control. Navy ships **patrol** the waters. Sailors make sure other ships can travel safely.

U.S. NAVY BASES

The Navy has bases all over the world. Some bases are used for training. Other bases get supplies to ships on missions.

Getting Information

The Navy also gathers information on enemies. The MQ-4C Triton is a good tool for that. This drone carries cameras and **radar**. It allows sailors to see enemies. This drone can also track communications. Sailors can tell where messages are coming from.

The MQ-4C has a top speed of **358 miles** (576 km) per hour.

Rescues

Navy sailors do daring water rescues. They aid pilots who have crashed. They pick up people on sinking ships.

The Navy also delivers food and supplies to people in need. After natural disasters, sailors help wherever they are needed.

U.S. NAVY

By the Numbers

336,978

total active duty sailors in 2019

6

number of U.S. presidents who served in the Navy

18,000

meals prepared each day for sailors on the USS *Theodore Roosevelt*

1775

year the U.S. Navy began

CHAPTER 4

Ships and Subs

The Navy uses several seacrafts. Attack submarines seek and destroy enemy subs. They also destroy enemy ships. U.S. Navy subs carry missiles and **torpedoes**. Subs fire the weapons while still hidden deep underwater.

Life in a sub is not easy. Subs stay underwater for months at a time. Sailors don't have windows to look out. And they have almost no **privacy**.

AIRCRAFT CARRIERS

Carriers are huge. The Navy relies on them for big missions. More than 5,000 crew members ride on some carriers.

CATAPULTS
FLIGHT DECK
HULL

Comparing Naval Sizes

China

Iran

North Korea

United States

total ships
(as of 2018)

Destroyers

Destroyers are another type of Navy ship. Destroyers often travel with aircraft carriers. Weapons on destroyers protect carriers. But some destroyers can also attack enemies from a distance. The Zumwalt destroyers have missiles. These missiles can shoot targets in the air.

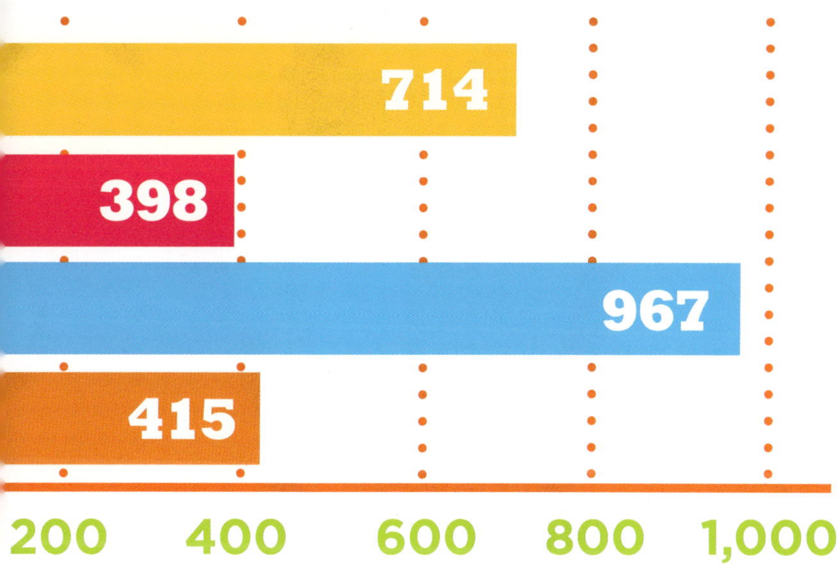

Always Prepared

U.S. Navy sailors are always prepared. They launch aircraft into battles. They destroy enemy watercraft. They do all they can to protect the United States.

304
LCDR P. J. ZETTEL
"McD"
HOT

conflict (KON-flikt)—an extended struggle or battle

engineer (en-juh-NEER)—a designer or builder

nuclear reactor (NOO-clee-ur ree-AK-tur)—a large device that produces nuclear energy; nuclear energy is created by splitting atoms.

patrol (puh-TROHL)—going around an area to make sure it is safe

privacy (PRAHY-vuh-see)—the state of being away or private from others

radar (RAY-dar)—a device that sends out radio waves for finding the location and speed of a moving object

recruit (ri-KROOT)—a newcomer to a group or field of activity

territory (TER-uh-tor-ee)—a geographic area belonging to or under the control of a governmental authority

torpedo (tawr-PEE-doh)—a bomb shaped like a tube that is fired underwater

LEARN MORE

BOOKS

Boothroyd, Jennifer. *Inside the US Navy.* US Armed Forces. Minneapolis: Lerner Publications, 2018.

Mitchell, P. P. *Join the Navy.* US Armed Forces. New York: Gareth Stevens Publishing, 2018.

Sherman, Jill. *U.S. Navy.* Serving Our Country. Mankato, MN: Amicus, 2019.

WEBSITES

The Official Website of the United States Navy
www.navy.mil/

US Government for Kids: United States Armed Forces
www.ducksters.com/history/us_government/united_states_armed_forces.php

U.S. Navy & American Navy Recruiting
www.navy.com/

INDEX